www.finishinglinepress.com

The Science of Unvanishing Objects

poems by

Chloe N. Clark

Finishing Line Press
Georgetown, Kentucky

The Science of Unvanishing Objects

ACKNOWLEDGMENTS

Many thanks to the editors, staff, and readers of the following magazines
where some of these pieces first appeared:

Missing Girl Found— in *Outlook Springs*
Filed Under Hazy Creatures in *Stone Boat*
Echo(de); The Double Dark Theory of the Universe; Twistings in
Pidgeonholes
When Everyone Else Says After in *Soft Blow*
Google Search History, Tell Me Who I Am; An Infinity of Chip Bros; Tricks
to Keep Away the Dark; Ball Don't Lie; What the Earth Returns to Our
Mouths in *Hobart*
We Who Vanish in *Prick of the Spindle*
The Detective, Years After; Metal Lark in *Abyss&Apex*
These Dreams Your Children Grow in *Glass*
A Spell that Uses the Blood of Oranges; The Apparitionist in *Split Lip
Magazine*
The Body Turned in *Bombay Gin*
Turtles & Hares in *Vending Machine Press*
Error Coding in *(b)oinkzine*
Shells in *Midwestern Gothic*
After the Ikiryoh in *Sleet*
Rolling Dice in *Apex*
Missing Girls, Continued in *Public Pool*

Publisher: Leah Maines
Editor: Christen Kincaid
Cover Art: Chloe N. Clark
Author Photo: Chloe N. Clark
Cover Design: Elizabeth Maines McCleavy

Printed in the USA on acid-free paper.
Order online: www.finishinglinepress.com
              also available on amazon.com

Author inquiries and mail orders:
Finishing Line Press
P. O. Box 1626
Georgetown, Kentucky 40324
U. S. A.

Table of Contents

Missing Girl Found—

dead

or

missing girl found alive

or

missing girl found living in Paris, in New York City, in Rio de
Janeiro, in Hollywood, in Wonewoc, Wisconsin, because she'd
always appreciated alliteration

or

missing girl found to be unhelpful, psychics say, shaking their
heads, "it's as if she doesn't want to be found"

or

missing girl found to be the last goddamn straw to woman who
moves away because the town is turning, changing, becoming
some place unrecognizable

or

missing girl found underwater

or

missing girl found to have been abducted by aliens, bandits, a
coven of witches

or

missing girl found wanting

or

missing girl found to have been loved by her family and now
her mother sometimes curls into her daughter's bed during the
day, struggling to inhale her secrets, or even just the scent of her
shampoo dug deep into pillows

or

missing girl found beautiful, years later, by someone seeing her
photograph as they page through an old yearbook and know
nothing of her except that she was beautiful

or

missing girl found seven years later, released from faerie and
imagining nothing has changed

or

missing girl found to have kept a dream journal, the last entry: I
was underwater, at first scared, and then knew, somehow, I was
meant to be there, I was part of the water, the river, the rush that
keeps it moving
                                or
missing girl found to have never existed at all
                                or
missing girl found to be happy
                                or
missing girl found to be missed
                                or
                                or
                                or

Filed Under Hazy Creatures

They lived above me, those two
and spent the days leaning over
the balcony, watching the parking
lot. I'd walk the dogs

below them. The dogs nails clicking
against the pavement. They'd lean
over more, gaze on the dogs

and once I heard them talking.
"What is that do you think?" asked
one. The other, the one with
the band t-shirts always on, replied,
"I think it's like a wolverine."

The first craned his neck out more,
staring at the dogs, "no, dude,
because that would make it, like,
half cat."

I will remember this years later
and catch myself willing to
believe that sight can make
such errors—this
bestiary of the false.

Echo(de)

My heart is in my throat

        my heart   is   in   my   throat
I can break this down to its parts: that I am feeling my pulse
stronger, that my muscles are tensing
        I can know that my heart is not actually in my throat

but   when I saw the news today, I remembered that you don't
live that far from there, that you
live so close to something horrific, but you reminded me often
enough that no matter where you went you were living close to
something horrific, that life for you was always just this side of
something awful happening
        that everywhere here can be unsafe and I didn't know if
here meant this country or this world or maybe the universe itself

And on the news, I couldn't bear to watch it and I couldn't bear to
not watch it and I couldn't bear that these were my choices
        and my pulse is beating in my veins and you are in my
head, always, some memory of you   and my heart is
pounding until my breath hurts to be taken   You
said once that you loved the world best before you knew it at all

And when I try to sleep I count my heart beats instead of sheep
and each breath I take is like a weight on my chest and I am
saying please to the universe over and over though neither of us
ever believed in that sort of thing and   still
always   when I think of you
        my heart   is in   my throat

When Everyone Else Says After

The phone rings, trilling
field of crickets, and

She still runs to pick
it up, breathless "hello"

And it's never for her,
anymore, and she holds it out

To her mother, father,
sister, or hangs up "wrong number"

At night she dreams deep
of her best friend, sitting

On a stone-strewn lake
shore. She is gathering

Pebbles, piling them up
on her lap, glistening

Against her dark-washed
jeans. Her best friend

Picks up one, small and round
and white as snow cones before

The syrup drench, and she
places it in her mouth. She

Swallows it, one gulp, and
says it's for "safe-keeping."

Google Search History, Tell Me Who I Am

Sheed coach
Why isn't Sheed a coach?
Stats for Rasheed Wallace's time as Assistant Coach
Andrew Lincoln Abraham Lincoln
When I was a child I thought
What color are cubras?
What color are cobras?
myself foolish for believing
Can I feed my sour sugar?
What will happen if I feed my sour sugar?
What will happen if I feed my sour dough starter sugar?
that someone lived inside the mirror, waiting
How many people have broken their teeth testing gold?
to get out
Houdini
gif of pie
video of baby sloths in onesies
to get out, isn't that what we all fear
Fear of trees
Fear of books
Fear of dreams
Oneirophobia
How many people suffer from oneirophobia?
but what it was was that it would get out
Particle Physics
and understand so much more than me
Particle Physics Wikipedia
would never need to lose hours
Loss of time syndrome?
looking down one path that leads to another path
Fear of shadows word
sometimes the mirror flickers
What were mirrors originally made of?
sometimes I think I'm the one
Specific word for sense of taste

I'm the one looking out
Fibonacci sequence illustrated in nature
I'm scared
Sounds under water
I'm scared
Of darkness
Where does the word darkness come from?
Words for shadows
that this is all we are
Pictures underwater viewing the sky

The Double Dark Theory of Our Universe

I too believe that our lives are
not as interwoven as we are led to
believe, that you and I were
only coincidences in the others
timeline. Still, something

as simple as the entanglement
of our fingers reminds me that
once I felt entirely safe within
your world. Do you often, also, think

about black holes? How they taste
and swallow all the stars in their
path? Sometimes, when I see
you in a crowd, and I pretend
not to, I remember the way you

looked the last night I saw you
and you said in another life
we would be happy. And I said
in another life we would be

free from one another's ghosts.

A Breath Expelled

I never told you that I spend my nights chasing demons
    because I thought you'd say that was passé, that demon-chasing
was for teenage girls
        or men with too much time on their hands
And the demons I know are the ones with bad credit
    and they're easy to find, they hang out in the downtown diner
where you can get
        midnight stacks of pancakes slathered in too much
butter for less than two dollars
The first demon I saw was when I was in college and someone bent my
fingers
    back until they snapped but when I tell people this they only
ever say
        "oh that explains why your pinky is so crooked."
So I never told you that sometimes I even chase them in my sleep
    because I thought that you'd say that I needed to let go, that
dreams
        of demons were holding me back
And the demons I dream are the ones with low voices
    who wear tight jeans and lean over me in cafes to ask what I'm
reading
        and, you know, in dreams I'm always reading the same
dumb book
The first demon I tracked was the one who kept the names of the dead
    tattooed on his skin and he liked to go shirtless,
        show off how the names moved, how they wept when
the sun hit them
But I never told you that I know my demons
    because I thought you'd find that strange, that I would keep
them
        curled in my mind, a sense memory of what not to do
And the demons I know are the ones I can deal with
    because they're easy to spot, with their shining eyes
        and their fingers always just slightly too thin
The first demon I met was just like them all and
    now I know what to look for, know to let you speak first
        and I will cast them from your body if you let me

We Who Vanish

I say to him that Jean Robert-Houdin once made a tree
blossom into life. Houdini took his name
from him. And Steven Millhauser used that trick
for his Eisenheim. And I'm thinking about how that tree must
have felt springing upwards as the wind-up butterfly
swam circles through the air.

He changes the subject, says he dreamed my feet
were bleeding. I've been doing a lot of
walking. The soles of my shoes are worn almost
smooth and so my footprints seem blank. Sometimes
I walk to the café to order hot chocolate with shots
of espresso and I try to sit and just sit but my feet
keep tapping the floor. I've seen tigers pace cages
at zoos and I wonder if this is why— their bodies still
hold the memory of the walking they've done and it courses
through their blood like some impossible
musical beat that they can never quite catch up to.

He tells me I'm doing it again like when he asked
me about my religion as if it was something as concrete
as mathematics: addition, subtraction, a Fibonacci sequence
of devotion. I said that poets have found death in a handful
of dust or seen hell collapse behind them step
by step. They do not tell me of heaven because there is no
space for it. I said that there are prayers even
to say upon witnessing lightning. That flash
of light burned imprints on my eyes
and for days I saw it and thought I was witnessing
the divine. I once was blinded by the sun reflected
on a lake. I once was lost. But now I'm— I said that
I don't always trust my image in mirrors. I said I've
never been in love but I've fallen for love. I've counted
up beads and thrown salt over my shoulders and held
my breath when passing graveyards. I said that I've touched
light bulbs still hot and it felt just the same
as trying to explain.

He sighs and says go back to magic and so I do, I think
that if I had been there then, some audience member
in from the cold, I would
have watched with breath held. And when that tree
unfurled and the butterfly danced out to us,
well I think right then I might
have believed in anything.

The Detective, Years After

Missing women often appear
to me in dreams, always asking

the same questions: why it was her
that I had found instead of them,
why she was the one brought home

alive, fighting
the twisting, a rush
that crept up through her body.

Years later, she would say to me:
*Most days, I think I will start
screaming and never stop.*

The wind will sometimes wake me
from dreams, inciting the trees
outside to tap codes onto my windows,
Morse message pleas for me to stir,

and the women will be waiting
at the foot of the bed or standing
by the window or leaning over me
to whisper secrets in my ears—
locations of their bodies,

the depth of dirt that presses down on them,
the feel of decomposition
—and I never know
how to tell them I am sorry
I stopped looking.

The missing women ask me why I never
found them; I try to answer
but words come out

sounding only like the crush of dead leaves
under foot as I searched.

Twistings

The first time I see my love unclothed
he looks like the vanity mirror version
of what I'd imagined:

everything just a little different
than I expected. Sharper angles
and a scar that wound

down one leg, a shooting star
arc of once-felt pain. His body
I imagined would fit into

mine so easily, like threading
a needle through my desire. Up
close, there was one small flaw

in his consistency: a dark circle
in his center, where a belly button
might have been there was a just

an absence. I asked him what it was,
what it meant, and he told me that
when he was born his mother forgot

to give him a name. He told me
to kiss him, close my eyes, and taste
his skin on my tongue. He tasted like

the lake where I swam as a child,
the color of the sky before storms,
the feeling of falling from a hammock

but before the wind got knocked from
my lungs. Those split seconds before
the gasp, the whoosh of pain, always

felt like this time I might
become unmade.

These Dreams Your Children Grow

My mother told me I was born in the night
sky, falling through space like a tiny wailing
comet and for years, you know, I believed

in her. I saw the stars beneath my skin, veins
shimmering milky way heart beating. Older,
I grew suspicious, the sky seemed so far

far away. And though I could taste the moon
on the tip of my tongue it was like a taste
foreign and unaccustomed: spices I've never
been able to gain the trust of.

A lover once pressed body into mine, said
your pulse sounds like planets exploding—
so distant and small and unremarkable
for such a tremendous thing.

When I call my mother on the phone, I ask
if she can tell me what the sky looked
like when I was born and she says: it was
the color of your eyes, deep as ocean dark.

And once upon a time, I had a dream
I was drowning and no one heard me
screaming and the water filled my lungs

and the pressure was too great and the sky
was inside out and my mother woke me
up, told me to study the night.

Outside my window, the sky
was filled with light, thousands of stars
calling me home or telling me to stay.

An Infinity of Chip Bros

On the bus, crunched between
the pole and an undergrad, I try to study
my hands. It's easy to forget
the lines our own palms contain:
whirls and patterns that make us
us. When my ears tune into
the conversation between one
standing undergrad and the one
sitting next to me:
>   "Did you remember your lunch today?"
>   "Got some Cool Ranch Doritos."

A woman gets on the bus in bright red
scarf, down coat, a reminder that ice
is coming, watching my breath roll
out of my mouth, waiting, is coming.
>   "Oh, man, yeah, you like
>   your chips."
>   "No, just Doritos.
>   Cheetoes, Fritos,
>   I hate that shit, but I love me some
>   Doritos."

Across the street, from through
the window, there is a man running,
to catch his daughter who has gotten
free of held hands, of the safety of
someone keeping her near, and I
hope he can catch her, but the bus
turns before I see.
>   "No Fritos?" The sitting one says, pain palpable
>   in his voice.
>   "You know she tried to pack me some once
>   and I brought them back and she said, 'I could've
>   given you something else.' And I said, 'yeah, well,
>   you should have."

We are twelve stops away
from my stop and my watch says
I'm almost late. If you're always early,
then you're on time, someone told me
once. And maybe my watch is fast,
maybe I'll be there on time, maybe—
                    "Did you miss your stop?"
                    "No, the bus stops closer. I mean
                    normally I'm all about the walking,
                    like I'm a walker, but not
                    in these shoes and it's fucking cold
                    as shit."
But things that come from the body
are never cold, I want to say, catching
my tongue. There are only so many
conversations I have ever wanted to get
into. And he's wearing leather boating
shoes, dark, barely worn, warm.
                    "Headed to the comp sci building?"
                    "Yeah, you know it."
                        "Class?"
                    "No, just hanging with my homies."
                            Silence.
                    "Just hanging with my homies."
                            Silence
                    "But, also, like class."
The bus stops, one leaves,
and I am back to silence or,
at least, the absence of over-
heard conversations. Everyone
returns to the screens of their
phones. Outside the bus, the fog
is rolling in, it looks like
the ghost of a blanket, reminding
that there used to be something
to keep me warm.

A Spell with the Blood of Oranges

There is a magic trick that no one really knows how to do.

> It's the one where the magician drowns at the end and the
> audience rushes the stage and resuscitation is attempted and the
> magician doesn't make it.

The man I loved had the build of an escape artist. He taught me how to
slip

> from handcuffs, from the borders of maps, from graves. He
> showed me how to place my feet and palms on the bed and raise
> my body like I was overcome with the spirit of god.

Once a girl threw herself off the top of a thirty story building because her
lover was a high-wire artist.

> He had been the best in the world and everyone said his ability
> to balance was supernatural. I saw him once and imagined that
> the people who loved him must also hate him.

When the man I loved disappeared, I looked for him in unexpected
places. I checked under cars,

> in the back of hotel room closets, and even in the least used
> stacks of college libraries—the untranslated French poetry
> collections and the books made up of superstitions.

The girl didn't die and the story made all of the newspapers. She broke
every bone

> in her body but somehow she lived and the press heralded it
> as a miracle. She made a statement: I am more than him now.
> He is no miracle. Later, she died of her internal injuries and the
> obituary was kept to the back pages.

Sometimes, without warning, I faint. Sometimes, after, I will wake up in places

> I don't remember ever having been. The smell of oranges, of cinnamon, of cloves, will be in the air. I will taste cocoa ground with chili peppers on my tongue. When people ask me if I'm alright, I never know how to respond.

There is a magic trick that no one really knows how to do.

It's the one where the magician's assistant is locked into a mirror. She pounds and pounds on the glass but no one ever knows the words to bring her back on through.

Ball Don't Lie

In my dream last night, basketball was on
and Sheed was a three-point machine, shooting
half-court shots that were nothing

but net. Last year, I told my boyfriend
to watch his step on ice and when
did I get so protective, so quick to keep

everyone safe around me? Sheed was never
a three-point machine but he hit when
he needed to. Sheed was defense and

attitude and tattoos of the sun. On the phone,
I ask a friend if her husband is doing better,
if his dreams have gotten less filled

with terror. She tells me some nights
are better than others. And I think
that aging is often like that: we take

our better where we find it. When
Sheed was a Celtic and in the playoffs
that final year, I saw him clutch

his back, the pain clear on his face
and, I thought, some day, I will
understand this loss.

The Body Turned

He told me that it was what teeth
were made for: the tearing, the pull.
We were made to devour.

I think of you most when I'm falling
asleep on boats in the middle
of the ocean and I remember
that some people even eat
squid, the ink blackens
their teeth, and some eat
lions, and tigers, and bears,
oh my.

He told me that my hands were made
for searching, he could read it in the lines
stretched taut across my palms, little
trip wires of the life laid out before
me. He said I should stop, give
in, and taste something hot
and sharp on my tongue.

I think of flesh and muscle and bones
and veins and the pulsing beat
of a heart. It reminds me of the taste
of ash, of the memory of dust,
of the color of the eyes of the man
I was meant to marry in the ghost story
dream I used to have.

He told me that meat is sweetest,
caught fresh, and from something
wild. He said you could taste
the freedom in the flesh.

I think of a deer running,
the trees made blur, and the sun
dipping low enough to kiss, and the deer
runs and runs. I remember the sound
of the mother deer calling out, rage
and loss, as the coyotes circled the twins.
She scared them away with her yell, those
wild dogs sent away.

He told me he could taste the freedom,
sweet upon his tongue, and I stare out
the window, watching the sun bleed
into the forest.

What the Earth Returns to Our Mouths

we have eaten dirt, still clinging
to the beets we thought we washed

clean, so careful, so impossible
to get every bit

                    And there is nothing we can do for
                    you, say the birds, pecking at our skin

                    they think we taste as sweet as candy
                    canes, as overripe pawpaw fruit

we have been eating so much
earth, it sticks between our teeth

rich and dark and even our
hair grows silky with the clay

                    And there is nothing we will do for
                    you, say the roots of trees, pushing

                    through our bones, up and up,
                    as if our ribs are ladders

we try to remember to clean,
clean the skin, until it bleeds

red into the lines of our hands,
this color, it looks so familiar

Turtles and Hares

There once was a woman
who found skulls buried
beneath sand, she was looking
for seashells and found molars,
incisors, sockets where hazel
eyes once were. She unearthed
them gently—she feared a skull
might disintegrate as easily as the once
lived in shell of a horseshoe crab.

A boy chose to swallow a key.
He felt it unlocking the bones
of his trachea. It tasted of
metal but also of divinity—
that sugary candy foam his mother
once stirred above the stove for
what seemed like hours.

There was a village where one
of every family lived. They gathered
the bones of their loves and buried
them three feet deep. The key
swallowed by one fell through
the bones of a ribcage and turned
eventually to rust and then to nothing
ever again to be found.

Error Coding

301 Moved Permanently
Your body still an arc, a part of this curve we called our own
When I miss you most it is in the memory of your walk or the way
you stretched your calf muscles out by balancing on different points
of your feet or the scar across the back of your hand, the white ridged
skin tattoo you never chose
502 Bad Gateway
Remember that house we looked at in a city we didn't live in?
It was open and the realtor led us through with a smile. You
whispered: imagine who we'd be if we lived here. And I said: if we
lived here, we'd be home now. But maybe you'd never seen those ads,
because you only said yes.
530 Site is Frozen
Winter came early and you watched your breath leave your mouth
You said you wondered if there was a word for people who read
fortunes in the shapes made by breath
You said it was so cold you could taste it
You told me to try and tell you what it reminded me of
451 Redirect
The wine was the color of a bad bruise. It seemed like it only existed
to stain: lips, furniture, the white dress I wore because I'm an idiot.
You spent the night talking to everyone else and I didn't know anyone
so I stood in corners and tried to smile
444 No Response
The phone ringing in the other room. In the car, music on, that one
song we listened to over and over. Knocking on the door.
100 Continue
Later, I will think of the conversations we started. The ones
interrupted. When you were explaining
something to me. Or I was telling you about
the dream I had. Something always
came up. And there is just this
now: the unfinished.

300 Multiple Choices

In the dream I never finished telling I was taking a test in a classroom without windows. My childhood best friend stood in front of the room, playing with a slinky. She said, Jesus Christ, have you ever tried to make these things go backwards?

And I broke down crying, unable to keep filling out the bubbles on my sheet of paper. I wasn't sad or frustrated or angry and the tears tasted like rainbow sherbet.

103 Checkpoint

Your hands. Your mouth. The weight of your body. These specifics that add up to a person are what we dwell on after the loss. That the lips on mine will never again be your lips, your hands on my skin, the press of a body into mine will never again be yours.

520 Unknown Error

We can trace everything to its roots. It's what we are especially good at.

Yet

still

we can not find any explanation here.

Metal Lark

Let the birds scatter
themselves, wings clicking
like beads strung loose
upon a thread, and realize

that there are still some colors
we cannot make from jars. If
feathers can scratch, sculpted
fine from metals, then how

many will it take to build
the bird? Wind up the key,
turn a thousand times or more,
and let loose the clockwork

nightingale. Place paper
nests amongst the highest
tree branches, eventually
they will be filled

with marbles like eggs.

The Apparitionist

I used to sleep with this guy who studied Japanese ghosts in literature. He'd talk about them while I was trying to go to sleep and the names stuck in my head long after I'd forgotten his. *Shogo, Yokai, Yurei.* And his dog was named Lafcadio, I do remember that. The guy's name was something easy, one syllable, started with an L or a J.

I have an ex whose own ex before me attempted suicide. He said that *she cut along the horizon rather than up the mountain.* I asked what led her to it and he couldn't remember, but he thought that it might have been because she lost the ability to dream after a car accident. I took this metaphorically, but he corrected, said literally. Said she closed her eyes and nothing came. I was terrified for years afterwards that every bump on the head might sever my dreams from my body.

My best friend and I, when we were children, would chase ghosts down by the valley stream. We'd pass their names between us in the form of stories. There were so many tales we had memorized. Most were cannibalized, stolen from the memories of other towns. *The Dead Bride, The White Woman, The Lost Girl.* When we tired of the dead, we would catch tadpoles in cupped palms, just for a second before releasing them. Years later when the bodies of birds were found, I tried to imagine them back to life and I would always get as far as their lives inside eggs.

I had a cousin who sold her soul, or that's what she told me. She said the devil met her at a game of cards. She said the devil was a beautiful woman. She said the devil spoke in French and she didn't speak the language, so she thought she was merely selling the memory of a man she once knew. And what does it feel like to have no soul, I asked. *Like every night is the night before Christmas but you never wake up on Christmas morning,* she told me.

There was a woman who I knew. She had a scar that perfectly circled her body, as if she had once been sawed in half. *I've never liked that magic trick,* she told me once in confidence. I never saw the scar, though, she told me about it as if one day I would and she didn't want me to be surprised.

My friend reads the shapes of people's skulls. She brushes out my hair, takes bobby pins, and begins to pull it all into swoops. Her fingertips on my scalp map out the secrets of my fortune. When I lean backwards and rest fully into her hands, she says that she knows my future. You will carry such heavy things. I laugh, thinking the voice she has adopted is merely theatrical until she continues. *You will carry so many other people's ghosts.*

Tricks to Keep away the Dark

We've been eating oranges
until our mouths go numb

sticky juice coats our
hands, our lips

sweet and sour and

we've been told that citrus
keeps the spiders away,

the moths from cupboards
and the ghosts from

under the bed,
sliding out incorporeal

shadow-long fingers
reaching up to tangle

in our hair, but no
longer, we spit orange

seeds onto wooden floors,
run our hands down

each other's bodies

proofing the skin against
the touch of the dead

we feel safe when we
taste one another

and we feel safest
when our mouths are numb

Shells

Every year there is a month
in Iowa when the bodies
of cicadas litter the sidewalks

to be crunched underfoot movie
theatre popcorn style always
on their backs inward crossed

legs and wings folded so neat and
we have all been taught by our mothers
not to handle the dead as if it is something

that stains but remember how once
we kept the shells cicadas crawled from
after seventeen years in slumber and how

we thought that they looked like jewels
hollowed out amber and we kept them
until they crumbled or were lost or

simply disintegrated and we wonder
if the bodies too can be kept like that
a reminder to wake up

Stages of the Exorcism

it is natural, instinctual even, to blame

the unknown for failure of crops, the work
of witches and so, too, the deaths of children

stories for protection,
rituals against the dark

the weight
of loss, the shape of something removed

salt thrown over shoulders
breath held past graveyards

rules given to monsters

Rural Routes in Iowa

When the car breaks down on some rural road
in the middle of Iowa and I'm telling Lee
to just calm down for five seconds
         and then I see a sign, markered on cardboard,
         LAST CHANCE TO KNOW YOUR FUTURE and
         the price is there too: $5.00. The zeroes look like
         sideways eyes, but I don't know why I think that.
         There's a stand
and a woman leaning against it. She's got hair
in scarf and bright colored skirt and, I swear
         on the hand of God, that she has hoop earrings. She'd
be pretty if this
         was a movie. But she just looks sad. I go up to her,
place a five on the
         table with a smack.
She takes my hand in her hands, runs a long
fingernail all over my palm in slow, concentric
circles that makes me miss sleepovers
         as a girl. My friends and I would brush out each
other's hair, make braids
         tight, and there is something so soothing in having
someone else run
         fingers through
your hair. The woman shakes her head, hands
back my money, says: lady, you have no fortune,
and I laugh, say: what the fuck?
         She shrugs and Lee yells that the car is running. And
I go back to him,
         again. But, she's right, when I think about it because I
haven't had palm
         lines for years.

After the Ikiryoh

Read, read to me, the letters that you wrote
me when I was young and you were tender,
sweet, your touch was soft then, caressed
my skin, made me ache and arch my body,

the bridge to your river.
In the river I am filling my lungs with algae
emeralding tendrils stop, stopping my breath

You said you'd never not love me, well, they say
hate is love in mirrors, and you bent back my fingers
to touch my wrist, and your touch was quick then,
pulling, twisting, made me ache and arch my body,

the tree limbs under such weight.
The weight of your thoughts filling my body with ghosts
spiriting breath stop, stopping my heart

Speak, tell me, say again those words you spoke,
they dripped with demons, when I was young,
and you were harsh, your touch was pain then, clawed
my skin, made me ache and arch my body,

the bones under your hands.
Your hands pushing me down filling my head with nothing
hating thoughts stop, stopping my soul

Rolling Dice

Here's what I think about deals
with the devil. They're always
at night, on bridges, in the backroom of every house you
have ever lived. The devil
wears blue, black, red, shades of white.
The devil arrives and

Usually it's midnight, though
not always, when the words go
from lips to ears, ears to lips,
lips to lips. The devil always knows
how to say your name just
right, the way it makes your toes
curl, your skin burn, and

Sometimes the devil gives
you the chance to take it back,
just cross that bridge before
anyone else, swim to the bottom
of that bottomless lake, steal three golden
locks of hair. Yet, mostly,

It ends with the devil reaching
out, taking your hand, holding
you close, close, close, until
the sky falls out of your
skin, the waves break backwards, the taste of silver
on your tongue, until

The devil, and you, and you
make three.

Missing Girls, Continued

My best friend swallows needles
while we sit beside one another
in the dark, watching static

flicker on the television. She says
do you remember:

that boy in grade school who let
go of the merry-go-round? Someone
found his tooth embedded in concrete
days later. I say isn't it miraculous

we all survived childhood? She turns
to me and I see through her emptied
out eyes, all the way to the back

of her skull. Where does she store
her memories now, I wonder. And she
asks me if I think about when her parents

called me late at night and asked if I knew
where she was. I want to say: there is nothing
else that I think about more. But that's not

true. I often have the same dream, many
nights in a row, and in it we are staring
up at the night sky: counting all the shooting
stars that ice their way across the blue

but we forget to make wishes, too busy
thinking of how the stars must have
names, we just don't know how
to say them.

Additional Acknowledgments

Huge thanks to everyone at Finishing Line Press.

Over the course of writing these poems, the following people have provided support, guidance, friendship, conversation, inspiration, senses of humor, willingness for me to run ideas past, generally being awesome, and/or taste-testing my various recipes when I needed a break from writing:
Brontë Wieland, Stephanie Gunn, Lisa Koca, Erin Schmiel, Molly Backes, Philippe Meister, Samantha Kohnert, Marc Seals, Ron Wallace, Kelly Dwyer, Debra Marquart, Corrina Carter, Meghann Hart, Kristin Gulotta, Sara Doan, Maria Rago, Jennifer Hutchins, Tony Quick, Charissa Menefee, and everyone in the English Department at Iowa State University.

And with eternal gratitude and love: my parents, brothers, sister-in-law, nephews, Millie Hatch, family, and corgis.

www.ingramcontent.com/pod-product-compliance
Lightning Source LLC
LaVergne TN
LVHW051610080426
835510LV00020B/3215